Little Cakes and Cookies to Bake

Abigail Wheatley

Designed by Helen Edmonds & Emma Latham

Illustrated by Francesca Carabelli
Photography by Howard Allman

Recipe consultant: Catherine Atkinson
Food preparation by Maud Eden

Contents

Getting started

The tips on this page will help you to get to grips with some baking basics. Once you've read through them, you can start cooking.

Before you start

Before you start cooking, read the recipe carefully and check you've got all the ingredients and equipment you need. Then, wash your hands.

Food allergies

If you're cooking for someone with a food allergy or intolerance, this book will help you. Recipes that contain nuts are clearly marked. The ingredients lists show where allergy-free alternatives can be substituted. And on page 64 you can find out which recipes are suitable for allergy sufferers.

Weighing and measuring

The recipes show two different types of weights. Use either, but don't swap between them.

For some ingredients, you only need a pinch – the amount you can pick up between your thumb and first finger.

Small quantities

The recipes in this book often use very small quantities of ingredients. Because of this, you need to measure very accurately. Make sure you scrape all the mixture from the sides of your mixing bowls, too.

Your oven

All ovens are different – yours may cook things more quickly or slowly than the recipe says. If you're using a fan oven, shorten the cooking time or lower the temperature – the oven manual will help you with this.

Bake cakes and cookies in the middle of the oven. Arrange the shelves before you turn on the oven. Only open the oven door when the cooking time is up, or if you think something is burning.

Butter, margarine and spread

When a recipe says to use softened butter, leave it at room temperature for an hour before you start cooking. Only use margarines and spreads that say they are suitable for baking, and avoid 'low fat' types.

Measure small amounts with measuring spoons.

The ingredients should lie level with the top of the spoon.

Little cakes

Small strawberry sponge cakes – see page 12

On page 26 you'll find instructions for making decorations like these.

Find out how to make berry cupcakes on page 33.

This tiny cupcake (page 10) was topped with pink buttercream.

Little cake baking tips

Little cakes are often easier to make than big cakes, because you are handling smaller quantities. If you follow the tips here, your cakes should be perfect every time.

Cake sizes

Always use the size and shape of tin or paper case the recipe says, or your cakes might not turn out right. To find out how to grease and line tins and trays, see page 36.

Tiny paper cake cases

There are different sizes of tiny paper cake cases, so the number of cakes given in the recipe is only a guide. Tiny paper cases may flop during cooking. To prevent this, put a second case inside each one before you fill it.

Muffin tins

Some of the recipes in this section use a 6-hole deep muffin tin, but if you don't have one you can use a 12-hole one instead. Put the cake mix in the holes closest to the middle. Spoon a little water into the other holes, to stop the tin from overheating.

Using silicone

You can buy individual silicone cake cases in most sizes. These hold their shape on an ordinary, flat baking tray. Silicone cases can stick to cakes, so it's a good idea to grease them first (page 36).

Beating butter and sugar

1 Put the sugar and butter in a large mixing bowl. Stir them together with a wooden spoon.

2 Beat quickly with the spoon, until the mixture is pale and fluffy.

3 If the butter is hard to beat, pour hot water into a fresh bowl. Pour it out, dry the bowl, then transfer the mixture to it and try again.

Sifting

1 Put the ingredients in a sieve. Hold it over a bowl. Tap the sieve, so the ingredients fall through.

2 If there are lumps left in the sieve, squash them through with the back of a spoon.

Breaking eggs

Crack the egg sharply on the edge of a cup or small bowl. Pull the shell apart, so the white and yolk slide into the cup. Pick out any bits of shell.

Beating eggs

Beat the yolk and white with a fork, to mix them together well.

Mixing gently, or 'folding'

1 Use a big metal spoon. Move it gently through the mixture, making the shape of a number 8.

2 Stop as soon as everything is mixed together.

Is it cooked?

At the end of the cooking time, you need to test whether a cake is cooked. Take it out of the oven. Poke the middle of the cake gently with your finger. It should feel firm and springy. If it doesn't, bake for 5 minutes more, then test again.

Tiny cupcakes

Ingredients:

For the cupcakes:

40g (1½oz) caster sugar

40g (1½oz) softened butter, soft margarine or dairy-free spread

40g (1½oz) self-raising flour

1 medium egg

1½ teaspoons cocoa powder

1 tablespoon white chocolate chips

1 tablespoon milk chocolate chips

For the vanilla buttercream:

50g (2oz) softened butter, soft margarine or dairy-free spread

100g (4oz) icing sugar

1 teaspoon vanilla essence

For the chocolate buttercream:

50g (2oz) softened butter, soft margarine or dairy-free spread

75g (3oz) icing sugar

25g (1oz) cocoa powder

1 teaspoon milk or water

You will also need around 24 tiny paper cake cases, 2 baking trays and a piping gun or bag with a star- or flower-shaped nozzle.

Makes around 24

This recipe is for tiny vanilla and chocolate cupcakes topped with buttercream. You could decorate them with sugar sprinkles, melted chocolate and chocolate buttons.

1 Heat the oven to 180°C, 350°F or gas mark 4. Arrange the paper cases on the baking trays.

2 Put the sugar and butter, margarine or spread in a big bowl. Sift in the flour. Break the egg into a cup, then pour it in. Mix well.

3 Spoon half the mixture into another bowl. Sift the cocoa powder over it. Add the white chocolate chips. Mix. Put the milk chocolate chips in the first bowl. Mix.

4 Spoon the chocolate mixture into half the paper cases and the plain mixture into the others. Each case should be around two-thirds full.

5 Bake for 10-12 minutes, or until risen and firm. Leave the cakes for a few minutes, then put them on a wire rack to cool.

This cake was topped with a blob of buttercream, some melted chocolate and sugar strands.

If you use margarine or dairy-free spread in your buttercream, it's best to spread it onto your cakes instead of piping it.

6 While the cakes are cooling, make the vanilla buttercream, then the chocolate buttercream, following the instructions on page 14.

7 When the cakes are cool, pipe chocolate buttercream onto some and vanilla buttercream onto others, following the instructions for piping swirls on page 49.

8 If you want to scatter on sugar sprinkles or add chocolate buttons, do it straight away, while the buttercream is still sticky.

Small strawberry sponge cakes

Ingredients:

For the cakes:

75g (3oz) caster sugar

75g (3oz) softened butter, margarine or dairy-free spread

½ teaspoon vanilla essence

2 medium eggs

75g (3oz) self-raising flour

For the filling:

25g (1oz) softened butter, margarine or dairy-free spread

50g (2oz) icing sugar

½ teaspoon vanilla essence

4 tablespoons strawberry jam

For decorating:

2 tablespoons icing sugar

You will also need a 6-hole deep muffin tin.

Makes 6

These cakes are miniature versions of a popular cake often known as a Victoria sponge. They are filled with vanilla buttercream and strawberry jam.

1 Heat the oven to 180°C, 350°F or gas mark 4. Grease the inside of each hole of the muffin tin (see page 36) using a little softened butter, margarine or dairy-free spread.

2 Put the sugar and the butter, margarine or spread in a big bowl. Beat until you have a fluffy mixture. Add the vanilla.

3 Break one egg into a cup. Pour it into the bowl and mix. Do the same with the other egg. Sift over the flour and mix it in gently.

4 Spoon the mixture into the holes of the muffin tin. Bake for 20-25 minutes, or until firm and risen. Leave the cakes to cool for 10 minutes.

Run a knife around each cake if it's hard to get them out.

5 Hold the muffin tin upside down over a wire rack and shake, so the cakes pop out. Turn them the right way up again. Leave to cool completely.

6 While the cakes are cooling, use the butter, icing sugar and vanilla to make the vanilla buttercream, following the instructions on page 14.

7 When the cakes are cool, cut each one in half, like this.

8 Spread a little buttercream over each bottom half, then spread on some jam. Put the top halves back on.

9 To decorate the cakes, spoon the icing sugar into a small sieve. Hold it over each cake and tap it gently.

All these cakes were filled with strawberry jam, but you could use other flavours.

These cakes look pretty topped with a slice of strawberry.

Strawberry Jam

Icings and frostings

Here you'll find recipes and instructions for making icings and frostings. For some little cakes and cookies, you may need to make a smaller amount than the quantities given here – check the recipe, as it will tell you what quantities to use.

Chocolate buttercream

Chocolate buttercream

You will need 50g (2oz) softened butter, soft margarine or dairy-free spread, 75g (3oz) icing sugar, 25g (1oz) cocoa powder and 1 teaspoon milk or water.

1 If you're using butter, put it in a bowl. Beat until soft and fluffy. If you're using margarine or spread, just put it in a bowl.

2 Sift on half the icing sugar. Stir it in. Sift on the rest of the icing sugar and the cocoa powder. Add the milk or water. Mix well.

Chocolate chips

Vanilla buttercream

Vanilla buttercream

You will need 50g (2oz) softened butter, soft margarine or dairy-free spread, 100g (4oz) icing sugar, 1 teaspoon vanilla essence and 1 teaspoon milk or water.

1 If you're using butter, put it in a bowl and beat until it's soft and fluffy. If you're using margarine or spread, just put it in a bowl.

Raspberry buttercream – see page 17

2 Sift on half the icing sugar and stir it in. Then, sift on the rest of the icing sugar and add the vanilla and milk or water. Mix well.

Orange buttercream

Lemon buttercream

Citrus buttercream

For orange, lemon or lime buttercream, follow the instructions for vanilla buttercream (left) but at step 2 leave out the vanilla and milk or water. Instead, grate the zest from 1 orange or 1 lemon or 2 limes, then cut the fruit in half and squeeze out the juice. Add the zest and 2 teaspoons of the juice to the mixture. Mix well.

Chocolate frosting

You will need 40g (1½oz) butter (preferably unsalted) and 75g (3oz) plain or milk chocolate, broken into pieces.

1 Put the butter in a small pan. Put the pan over a low heat, until the butter melts. Take the pan off the heat.

2 Add the chocolate. Stir until it melts. If you're using the frosting as a cake topping or filling for sandwiching cookies, scrape it into a bowl and refrigerate for 20 minutes.

Glacé icing

You will need 100g (4oz) icing sugar, 2 teaspoons water and some food dye (optional).

1 Sift the icing sugar into a bowl. Mix in the water until you have a smooth, spreadable paste.

2 Mix in a few drops of food dye, if you like. Or, for more than one shade, divide the icing between separate bowls and mix a different shade into each.

Little chocolate cherry gateaux

Ingredients:

For the cakes:

50g (2oz) self-raising flour

20g (¾oz) cocoa powder

½ teaspoon baking powder

75g (3oz) softened butter, margarine or dairy-free spread

75g (3oz) caster sugar

2 medium eggs

½ teaspoon vanilla essence

1½ tablespoons milk or water

For the filling and topping:

150ml (¼ pint) double cream

4 tablespoons cherry jam

a block of plain chocolate

6 fresh cherries (optional)

You will also need a 6-hole deep muffin tin.

Makes 6

This recipe is for miniature chocolate cakes layered with cherry jam, whipped cream and grated chocolate. There are also suggestions for other flavours, opposite.

1 Heat the oven to 180°C, 350°F or gas mark 4. Grease each hole of the muffin tin (see page 36) using butter, margarine or dairy-free spread.

2 Sift the flour, cocoa and baking powder into a big bowl. Put the butter, margarine or spread and sugar in another bowl.

3 Beat the butter, margarine or spread and sugar until the mixture becomes pale and fluffy.

4 Crack an egg into a cup. Tip it into the butter and sugar mixture. Add 1 tablespoon of the floury mixture. Beat well. Do the same with the other egg, too.

Move the spoon in the...

...shape of a number 8.

5 Add the rest of the floury mixture, and vanilla and milk or water. Stir everything together gently, using a big metal spoon.

6 Spoon the mixture into the tin. Bake for 12-15 minutes, until risen and firm. Leave to cool for a few minutes.

Run a knife around each cake if it's hard to get them out.

7 Hold the tin upside down over a wire rack. Shake until the cakes pop out. Turn them the right way up. Leave to cool.

To make this version, don't cut your cake. Spread chocolate hazelnut spread around the sides. Roll it in chopped nuts. Spoon more spread on top. Decorate with a hazelnut.

A little chocolate hazelnut gateau

Don't beat too much, or the cream will go hard.

8 Whip the cream, following the instructions on page 54.

To make this little chocolate raspberry gateau, follow the instructions in the box below.

9 When the cakes are cold, cut them in half, like this. Spread some cream and then some jam on the bottom halves. Put the top halves back on.

A little chocolate cherry gateau

10 Spread more cream on the tops. Grate some chocolate over the tops, using the big holes on a grater. Put a cherry on each.

Little chocolate raspberry gateaux

For the filling and topping, you will need 100g (4oz) softened butter or dairy-free spread, 200g (7oz) icing sugar and 100g (4oz) raspberries. For the cakes, follow steps 1-7. For the raspberry buttercream, put the butter or spread in a bowl. Sift on the icing sugar, mash in 6 raspberries and mix. Cut each cake into 3 layers. Spread some buttercream on each one. Stack them up. Decorate with the remaining raspberries.

Mini éclairs

Ingredients:

For the éclairs:

40g (1½oz) plain flour

1 medium egg

25g (1oz) butter

For the vanilla cream:

½ teaspoon vanilla essence

1 tablespoon icing sugar

150ml (¼ pint) double or whipping cream

For the chocolate icing:

125g (4½oz) icing sugar

3 tablespoons cocoa powder

Makes around 8

Eclairs are cream-filled cakes with flavoured icing on top. Here you'll find out how to make mini chocolate, raspberry or coffee éclairs filled with vanilla cream.

1 Heat the oven to 220°C, 425°F or gas mark 7. Grease a baking tray with butter (see page 36). Hold the tray under a cold tap briefly, then shake off the water.

2 Cut out a large rectangle of baking parchment. Fold it in half. Unfold it again. Sift the flour onto it. Break the egg into a small bowl and beat it.

3 Cut the butter into small chunks. Put them in a pan with 75ml (3floz) cold water. Heat gently. As soon as it boils, take it off the heat.

4 Right away, fold up the parchment and tip the flour into the pan. Beat quickly for about a minute, until the mixture begins to form a ball in the middle of the pan.

5 Leave to cool for 5 minutes. Then, add a little egg and stir it in. Add the rest of the egg a little at a time, stirring well each time.

6 Put a teaspoon of the mixture onto the baking tray. Put on another teaspoon, touching the first one. Use the back of the spoon to smooth the blobs into a long éclair shape.

7 Spoon the rest of the mixture onto the tray in the same way. Make sure you space the éclairs well apart.

Don't beat too much, or the cream will go hard.

8 Bake for 10 minutes, then turn down the heat to 190°C, 375°F or gas mark 5. Bake for another 5-7 minutes, until they are puffy and golden-brown.

9 Use a spatula to move the éclairs onto a wire rack to cool. Carefully, make a hole in the side of each one with a sharp knife to let out any steam.

10 Pour the cream into a big bowl. Add the vanilla and sift over the icing sugar. Then, whip the cream (see page 54).

12 Cut the éclairs in half. Spoon vanilla cream into the bottom halves, then put the tops back on. Spread on some icing, following the instructions on page 48 for flat icing.

11 To make the icing, sift the icing sugar and cocoa into a bowl. Add 3 teaspoons warm water. Mix to make a spreadable paste. Add a little more water if it's too stiff.

Other flavours

For raspberry icing, squash 10 raspberries through a sieve. Mix the raspberry juice with 150g (5oz) sifted icing sugar.

For coffee icing, dissolve 2 teaspoons instant coffee in 3 teaspoons hot water. Mix in 150g (5oz) sifted icing sugar.

Tiny citrus cakes

Ingredients:

For the cakes:

1 orange or 1 lemon or 2 limes

100g (4oz) caster sugar

100g (4oz) softened butter, soft margarine or dairy-free spread

100g (4oz) self-raising flour

2 medium eggs

For the icing:

100g (4oz) icing sugar

You will also need around 40 tiny paper cake cases.

Makes around 40

This recipe is for tiny cakes flavoured with the juice and zest of lemons, oranges or limes. The cakes are topped with a layer of smooth icing.

1 Heat the oven to 180°C, 350°F or gas mark 4. Arrange the paper cases on two baking trays.

Only remove the outer layer – the white layer underneath tastes bitter.

2 Grate the zest from the outside of the fruit, using the small holes of a grater. Then, squeeze the juice from the fruit.

3 Put the zest, sugar and butter, margarine or spread in a bowl. Sift in the flour.

4 Break one egg into a cup, then pour it in. Do the same with the other egg. Add 2 tablespoons of the fruit juice. Mix everything together well.

5 Divide the mixture between the paper cases. Each paper case should be around two-thirds full. Bake for 10-12 minutes, or until risen and firm.

6 Set aside 3 teaspoons of the fruit juice for the icing. Spoon a teaspoon of the remaining juice onto each cake. Leave the cakes to cool.

These decorations were made by stacking two icing buttons (see page 27), then cutting them in half. You could put contrasting halves back together.

To make grapefruit-flavoured cakes, grate half the zest from a pink grapefruit, then cut it in half and squeeze the juice from one half.

Lemon and lime juice make white icing. To colour it, you could mix in a little yellow or green food dye.

7 While the cakes are cooling, make the icing. Sift the icing sugar into a bowl. Add the fruit juice you set aside. Mix to make a spreadable paste.

8 Spread some icing onto each cake. To make it really smooth, dip the blade of a blunt knife in warm water, then run it over the icing. Leave to dry a little before adding other decorations.

Little red velvet cakes

Ingredients:

For the cupcakes:

50g (2oz) caster sugar

25g (1oz) softened butter

1 rounded teaspoon runny honey or golden syrup

7 tablespoons plain natural yogurt

2 teaspoons red food dye

1 teaspoon vanilla essence

100g (4oz) plain flour

1 teaspoon bicarbonate of soda

1½ teaspoons cocoa powder

For the cream cheese frosting:

40g (1½oz) softened butter

75g (3oz) full fat cream cheese

250g (9oz) icing sugar

½ teaspoon vanilla essence

1 tablespoon lemon juice

You will also need 40 tiny paper cake cases.

Makes around 40

Red velvet cakes originated in America. These little red velvet cakes have a luxurious, velvety texture and contain a little liquid food dye to make them a rich, deep red.

1 Take the cream cheese out of the fridge. Heat the oven to 180°C, 350°F or gas mark 4. Arrange the paper cases on two baking trays.

Move the spoon in the...

...shape of a number 8.

2 Put the sugar, butter and honey or syrup in a bowl. Beat to mix them together well. Add the yogurt, food dye and vanilla and mix them in.

3 Sift on the flour, bicarbonate of soda and cocoa powder. Stir them in gently, using a big metal spoon.

4 Spoon the mixture into the paper cases. Each paper case should be around half full. Bake for 14-15 minutes, or until risen and firm.

Don't beat the cream cheese or it will go watery.

5 Leave the cakes for a few minutes, then put them on a wire rack to cool completely.

6 To make the frosting, put the butter and cream cheese in a bowl. Sift on the icing sugar. Add the vanilla and lemon juice. Mix gently.

Bow decorations

To make a bow decoration, you will need a cocktail stick and some ribbon.

Carefully cut the cocktail stick in half with scissors. Lay half the stick across the ribbon. Tie a half knot around the stick, then tie a bow. Slide the bow up to the cut end of the stick. Push the pointed end into a cake.

To make a bow decoration, follow the instructions in the box on the left.

These bows were made from red velvet ribbon.

Take out the bow decoration before you eat the cake.

7 Take the cases off the cakes. Use a knife to scrape the crumbs off the paper, until you have around 2 tablespoons of crumbs.

8 Put a sieve over a bowl. Push the crumbs through the sieve – use the back of a spoon to help them through.

9 Spread some frosting on each cake, making swirls and peaks with the knife. Then, sprinkle on some sieved crumbs.

Chocolate orange cakepops

Ingredients:

For the cake:

1 orange

40g (1½oz) softened butter, margarine or dairy-free spread

40g (1½oz) soft light brown sugar

1 medium egg

25g (1oz) self-raising flour

15g (½oz) cocoa powder

½ teaspoon baking powder

For the frosting:

25g (1oz) butter

50g (2oz) milk chocolate

For the coating:

200g (7oz) milk or white chocolate

sugar sprinkles and chocolate strands (optional)

You will also need 3 paper muffin cases, a 6-hole deep muffin tin and around 15 wooden skewers or lollipop sticks.

Makes around 15

Cakepops are little balls of cake on lollipop sticks. These cakepops are flavoured with chocolate and orange, and decorated with chocolate strands and sugar sprinkles.

1 Heat the oven to 180°C, 350°F or gas mark 4. Put the 3 paper cases in the muffin tin.

Only remove the outer layer – the white layer underneath tastes bitter.

2 Grate the zest from the outside of the orange, using the small holes of a grater. Then, squeeze the juice from half the orange. Save the zest for later.

3 Put the butter, margarine or spread and sugar in a bowl. Beat until you have a pale and fluffy mixture. Stir in 2 teaspoons of the orange juice.

4 Break an egg into a cup, then tip it into the bowl. Sift on the flour, cocoa and baking powder. Mix gently.

5 Spoon the mixture into the 3 paper cases. Bake for 12-15 minutes, until risen and firm. Leave for a few minutes. Then, move the cakes to a wire rack to cool.

6 To make the frosting, melt the butter in a small pan over a low heat. Take it off the heat. Break up the chocolate. Stir it in, until you have a smooth mixture. Stir in the orange zest.

7 When the cakes are cool, take off the cases. Crumble the cakes into a bowl. Keep on crumbling, until all the cake is in small crumbs. Mix in the frosting.

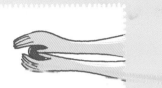

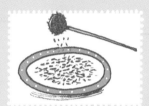

8 Scoop up a teaspoonful of the mixture. Roll it into a ball. Put it on a large plate. Make more cake balls the same way. Put the plate in the fridge for 30 minutes.

9 Pour some sprinkles onto a plate. Put out some cups or glasses to stand the finished cakepops in.

10 For the cakepop coating, melt the chocolate, following the instructions on page 55. Take a cakepop. Push a lollipop stick into the flattened part that was in contact with the plate.

11 Dip the cakepop in the chocolate. Spoon on more chocolate, to cover the cakepop. Hold it over the bowl and shake it gently, so any excess chocolate drips off.

12 Pick up some sprinkles with your fingers. Hold the cakepop over the plate and scatter sprinkles all over it. Stand the stick in a glass. Make more cakepops in the same way. Chill for 15 minutes, so the chocolate sets.

You could stand your cakepops in jam jars, or stuck into half oranges.

25

Making decorations

Here you can find out how to make your own little cake and cookie decorations from marzipan, chocolate paste and ready-to-roll icing.

Dyed marzipan or ready-to-roll icing

You will need some bought 'white' marzipan or white ready-to-roll icing and some food dye (for strong shades, use gel food dye). Marzipan contains nuts.

1 Take a golf-ball sized blob of marzipan or icing. Make a hollow in the middle. Drop in 3 or 4 drops of food dye.

2 Fold the marzipan or icing over the dye. Keep on folding and squashing until the dye is evenly mixed through.

A sprinkle-covered chocolate paste shape

Sprinkle-covered buttons

Icing balls

Chocolate paste

You will need 75g (3oz) plain or milk chocolate and 1½ tablespoons golden syrup.

1 Melt the chocolate (see page 55). Wearing oven gloves, take the bowl out of the pan.

2 Stir in the syrup until the mixture stops sticking to the sides of the bowl. Pat into a flattened ball.

3 Wrap in plastic food wrap. Put in the fridge for 1 hour. Take it out 10 minutes before you want to use it.

Rolling out and cutting

1 To roll out marzipan or ready-to-roll icing, dust a surface and a rolling pin with a little icing sugar. For chocolate paste, use cocoa powder instead of icing sugar.

2 Use the rolling pin to roll out the marzipan, icing or chocolate paste until it's around 2mm (⅛in) thick. Then, cut out shapes using tiny cookie cutters.

26

Buttons and balls

1 Take a little marzipan, ready-to-roll icing or chocolate paste. Use your hands to roll it into a ball.

2 To make a button, put the ball on a surface and flatten it with the back of a spoon.

An icing rose

A tiny cookie cutter was used to cut this leaf shape from rolled-out chocolate paste.

Roses

Roll out some marzipan, chocolate paste or ready-to-roll icing, so it's around 2mm (⅛in) thick.

1 Use a sharp knife to cut a strip 4cm (1½in) long and 1cm (½in) wide. Cut another strip the same length but only half as wide.

2 Put the narrow strip on top of the wide strip, against one of the long edges. Roll up both strips together, with the wide one on the outside. Pinch the solid base gently, to make it stick.

Sprinkle-covered shapes

You will need some marzipan, chocolate paste or ready-to-roll icing shapes, some sugar sprinkles and 2 teaspoons of icing sugar.

1 Put the icing sugar in a small bowl. Add ½ teaspoon of water and mix to a thin, smooth paste.

2 Brush or spread a thin layer of paste over the shapes. Scatter on some sprinkles. Leave to dry for at least 4 hours.

Iced fancies

For these fancy cakes, you bake a big cake, cut it into squares and ice them. You can make all your cakes lemon flavoured, or add a hint of rose to some of them.

1 Heat the oven to 180°C, 350°F or gas mark 4. Grease and line the cake tin (see page 36). Break the eggs into a bowl. Beat them with a fork.

Only remove the yellow layer – the white layer underneath tastes bitter.

2 Grate the zest from the outside of the lemons, using the small holes of a grater. Cut the lemons in half, squeeze out the juice and set it aside.

3 Put the zest, butter and sugar in a big bowl. Beat until pale and fluffy. Mix in a little beaten egg. Add the rest of the egg a little at a time, mixing well each time.

5 Bake for 25 minutes, or until risen and firm. Leave for a few minutes. Run a knife around the tin. Turn the cake onto a wire rack. Leave to cool completely.

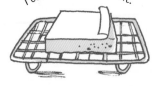

Peel off the parchment.

4 Sift on the flour. Add the milk. Mix very gently, using a big metal spoon. Spoon the mixture into the tin. Smooth the top with the back of a spoon.

Move the spoon in the...

...shape of a number 8.

6 Put the cake on a board. Cut off the crispy edges. Make 3 cuts across the cake, then 3 more in the other direction, to make 16 squares. Put them on a wire rack with a tray underneath.

7 Sift 175g (6oz) of the icing sugar into a bowl. Put half the butter in a pan. Add 2 tablespoons of lemon juice. Put the pan over a gentle heat.

The icing should be pourable. If it's too stiff, stir in a few drops of water.

8 When the butter melts, pour the mixture onto the icing sugar. Add a few drops of yellow food dye. Mix well.

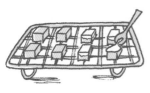

9 Spoon some icing onto half the cakes, covering the tops and letting it drip down the sides.

10 Sift the remaining icing sugar into a bowl. Put the rest of the butter in a pan. Add 5 teaspoons of lemon juice and 1 teaspoon of rose water. Heat as before, then pour onto the icing sugar.

11 Add a few drops of pink food dye. Mix well, as before. Ice the rest of the cakes. Decorate with piping (page 48) or decorations (page 26), if you like.

Lemon only

If you don't like rose flavour, you can make all your cakes lemon flavour instead. Follow steps 1-9 as normal. Then, follow steps 8-9 again, to ice the rest of the cakes.

Little coconut cakes

Ingredients:

For the cupcakes:

2 limes

65g (2½oz) butter or margarine

2 tablespoons desiccated coconut

75g (3oz) caster sugar

100g (4oz) self-raising flour

1 medium egg

2 tablespoons milk

For the lime frosting:

25g (1oz) softened butter

50g (2oz) full-fat cream cheese

175g (6oz) icing sugar

40g (1½oz) desiccated coconut

You will also need around 30 tiny paper cake cases.

Makes around 30

These little, moist cakes are made with a sweet and tangy combination of coconut and lime. They are topped in creamy frosting and then dipped in coconut.

1 Heat the oven to 180°C, 350°F or gas mark 4. Arrange the paper cases on two baking trays. Take the cream cheese out of the fridge.

Only remove the green layer – the white layer underneath tastes bitter.

2 Grate the zest from the outside of the limes using the small holes of a grater. Cut the limes in half and squeeze out the juice. Put half the zest in a big bowl.

3 Put the butter or margarine in a small pan. Heat gently until it melts. Then, take it off the heat.

4 Put the coconut and sugar in the bowl with the zest. Sift in the flour. Stir everything together.

These baking cups are made from thick paper. Use them like ordinary paper cases.

5 Break the egg into a cup and beat it with a fork. Pour it into the big bowl. Add the milk, the melted butter and 1 teaspoon of the lime juice. Mix well.

These curls of lime zest were made using a tool known as a zester.

6 Spoon the mixture into the paper cases. Each one should be two-thirds full. Bake for 10-12 minutes, or until risen and firm.

7 When the cakes are cooked, set aside 2 teaspoons of the lime juice for the frosting. Spoon the remaining lime juice over the hot cakes. Leave to cool.

8 To make the lime frosting, put the butter and cream cheese in a big bowl. Mix them together. Sift in half the icing sugar. Mix it in.

9 Sift in the rest of the icing sugar. Add the 2 teaspoons of lime juice you set aside earlier. Mix everything together.

10 Put the coconut in a small bowl. Spread some frosting on top of a cake. Hold the cake by the case and dip it in the coconut, to coat it.

11 Frost the rest of the cakes in the same way. Sprinkle the remaining lime zest over the cakes.

Upside-down berry cakes

Ingredients:

For the cakes:

2 oranges

100g (4oz) softened butter, soft margarine or dairy-free spread

100g (4oz) caster sugar

2 medium eggs

1 teaspoon gluten-free baking powder

100g (4oz) fine cornmeal (polenta)

6 large (or 12-18 small) fresh or frozen raspberries, blackberries or blueberries

For the berry icing:

100g (4oz) icing sugar

50g (2oz) smooth berry jam – use whatever flavour you like

For decorating:

a few fresh berries (optional)

You will also need a 6-hole deep muffin tin.

Makes 6

These moist upside-down cakes have berries in the middle and are topped with berry icing. The recipe is wheat- and gluten-free, and can be made dairy-free, too.

1 Heat the oven to 190°C, 375°F or gas mark 5. Grease the inside of each hole of the muffin tin (see page 36) using a little softened butter, margarine or dairy-free spread.

Only remove the outer layer – the white layer underneath tastes bitter.

2 Grate the zest from the oranges. Then, cut the oranges in half and squeeze out the juice.

3 Put the zest in a bowl. Add the butter, margarine or spread and the sugar. Beat until the mixture is pale and fluffy.

4 Break an egg into a cup. Beat it with a fork. Stir it into the mixture. Then, do the same with the other egg.

5 Add the baking powder and cornmeal and 2 teaspoons of the orange juice. Mix everything together gently.

6 Spoon the mixture into the holes of the muffin tin. Poke 1 large berry (or 2-3 small ones) into the middle of each one.

7 Bake for 20 minutes, or until firm and risen. Carefully, pour 2 teaspoons of orange juice over each cake. Leave to cool.

8 To make the icing, sift the icing sugar into a bowl. Add the jam. Mix it in until you have a smooth paste.

Run a knife around each cake if it's hard to get them out.

9 When the cakes are cold, put a board over the muffin tin. Turn the tin and board over together, so the tin is on top. Lift off the tin. Leave the cakes upside down.

10 Spoon some icing onto each cake. Top with the fresh berries.

Berry cupcakes

For berry cupcakes that aren't upside-down, bake the cakes in paper cases. At step 9, turn them the right way up, then spoon the icing on top. Or, pipe on swirls of buttercream – see page 15 for buttercream recipes and page 49 for piping tips.

Raspberry jam icing

Each of these cakes was topped with icing made from a different type of jam – strawberry, raspberry and blueberry.

33

Little cookies

Little gem biscuits – see page 42

These yoyo biscuits (page 46) were filled with buttercream.

Mini chocolate chip cookies – see page 60

On page 49 you can find out how to pipe decorations like these.

Little cookie baking tips

These tips will give you the skills you'll need to bake the delicious little cookies and biscuits in this section.

Greasing a tray or tin

1 Use a paper towel to scoop up a little softened butter or cooking oil.

2 Wipe the paper towel over the tin or tray, so it's thinly covered with butter or oil.

Separating eggs

1 Break the shell (see page 9). Let the white and yolk slide onto a small plate.

2 Cover the yolk with an egg cup. Hold the egg cup. Tip the plate over a bowl, so the white slides into the bowl.

Lining a tray or tin

1 Put the tin or tray on some baking parchment. Draw around it. Cut out the shape, cutting just inside the line.

2 If your mixture will touch the sides, grease the tin or tray first (see left). Then, put the parchment shape in the bottom of the tin or tray.

Beating egg whites

1 Beat the egg white very quickly with a whisk, until it becomes very thick and foamy.

2 Lift up the whisk. If the foam stays in a floppy point, you have whisked enough. Keep on whisking until it does.

Rubbing butter into flour

1 Stir the chunks of butter into the flour, to coat them. Pick up some butter and flour with the tips of your fingers and thumbs. Squash and rub them together, letting the mixture drop back into the bowl.

2 Carry on picking up the mixture, rubbing it and letting it fall back into the bowl. The lumps of butter will get smaller. Stop when they are the size of small breadcrumbs.

Using a rolling pin

1 Sprinkle a little flour over a clean work surface and a rolling pin. Put the dough on the surface.

2 Roll the rolling pin over the dough, going from the front to the back, then from the back to the front.

3 If you want a wide sheet of dough, turn the dough a quarter of the way around on the work surface. Roll over it again in the same way, to make it wider.

Hand heat

Some of the recipes tell you to use your hands to mix things. Pat and squeeze the mixture gently. The heat from your hands will help to bring the ingredients together.

Cookie cutters

Several of the recipes in this section use particular types of cookie cutters, but these are only suggestions. You can make your biscuits with any shape of cookie cutter you like.

1 Put a cutter over the rolled-out dough and press down gently, without twisting.

2 Lift up the cutter. If the dough shape comes too, hold the cutter over your baking tray and poke the shape, so it falls out. Otherwise, use a spatula to lift the shape carefully onto the baking tray.

Ginger biscuits

Ingredients:

50g (2oz) butter

50g (2oz) soft dark brown sugar

4 tablespoons golden syrup or runny honey

215g (7½oz) self-raising flour

3 teaspoons ground ginger

1 teaspoon ground cinnamon

¼ teaspoon allspice (optional)

For the icing:

100g (4oz) icing sugar

different shades of food dye (optional)

You will also need 2 baking trays, a rolling pin and some small heart-shaped (or other) cookie cutters.

Makes around 40

These crisp ginger biscuits are cut into hearts, but you could cut yours into any shape you like. They're decorated with pastel shades of glacé icing.

1 Heat the oven to 180°C, 350°F or gas mark 4. Line the baking trays with baking parchment (see page 36).

2 Put the butter, sugar and syrup or honey in a pan. Put it over a low heat until the butter melts. Take it off the heat.

3 Sift the flour, ginger, cinnamon and allspice into the pan. Stir well, to mix everything together. Put a lid on the pan and leave it to cool for 15 minutes.

4 Dust a clean surface and a rolling pin with flour. Take half the dough from the pan. Put it on the surface and roll it out (see page 37) until it's half as thick as your little finger.

5 Use the cutters to cut out lots of hearts and put them on the trays. Squeeze the scraps together, roll them out and cut more hearts.

6 Roll out the other piece of dough and cut it into hearts in the same way, too. Bake the biscuits for 8-10 minutes, until they're golden-brown.

7 Leave them on the trays for 5 minutes. Then, move them to a wire rack. Leave them to cool completely.

8 To make the icing, sift the icing sugar into a bowl. Mix in 2 teaspoons water, to make a smooth paste. Spoon some into two or more small bowls.

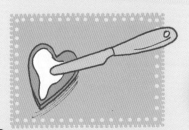

9 Put a few drops of food dye in each bowl. Mix well. Then, follow the instructions on page 48 to flat ice the biscuits.

Cook biscuits of the same size on the same baking tray. Smaller biscuits will cook in around 8 minutes, larger ones in around 10.

Shortbread fingers

Ingredients:

175g (6oz) plain flour

50g (2oz) rice flour or ground rice

1 teaspoon ground cinnamon

1 pinch ground nutmeg

125g (4½oz) butter, chilled

65g (2½oz) caster sugar

For the topping:

1 tablespoon caster sugar

100g (4oz) plain, milk or white chocolate

You will also need a 20cm (8in) square cake tin and a tray.

Makes 24

These chocolate-drizzled shortbread fingers are gently spiced with cinnamon and nutmeg. If you prefer plain shortbread, just leave out the spices.

1 Heat the oven to 150°C, 300°F, gas mark 2. Grease and line the tin (see page 36).

2 Sift the flour, rice flour, cinnamon and nutmeg into a big bowl. Cut the butter into chunks. Stir them into the flour mixture, to coat them with flour.

3 Use the tips of your fingers and thumbs to rub the butter into the flour, following the instructions on page 37. Stop when the mixture looks like small breadcrumbs.

4 Stir in the sugar. Then, use your hands to squeeze the dough, so it sticks together. Don't worry if there are a few loose crumbs.

5 Tip all the mixture into the cake tin. Use your fingers to push it into the corners and press it all down firmly. Level the top with the back of a spoon.

6 Mark 2 lines across the shortbread. Mark 7 lines in the other direction, to make 24 fingers. Bake for 35 minutes, until golden. Scatter over the caster sugar for the topping.

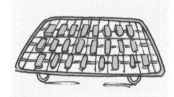

7 Leave in the tin for 5 minutes. Then cut the shortbread into 24 fingers, following the marks you made earlier. Cool for 5 more minutes, then move the fingers carefully to a wire rack to cool.

8 Line a tray with baking parchment (see page 36). When the fingers are cold, melt the chocolate (see page 55). Wearing oven gloves, take the bowl out of the pan.

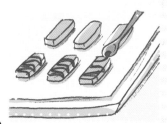

9 Arrange the shortbread fingers on the tray, spacing them out well. Drizzle over the chocolate, following the instructions on page 55.

10 Put the tray in the fridge for 15 minutes. The chocolate will set firm. Then, peel the fingers off the parchment.

Other flavours and ideas

To make lemon shortbread, leave out the spices. Add the finely grated zest of 1 lemon with the sugar in step 4.

For gluten-free shortbread, simply replace the flour with gluten-free flour.

Little gem biscuits

Ingredients:

20g (¾oz) icing sugar

40g (1½oz) softened butter, preferably unsalted

1 lemon

50g (2oz) plain flour

For the lemon buttercream:

25g (1oz) softened butter

50g (2oz) icing sugar

1 lemon

red and blue food dye

You will also need a baking tray and a piping gun or bag with a star- or flower-shaped nozzle.

Makes around 30

Each of these tiny, gem-like lemon biscuits is topped with a piped swirl of tangy lemon buttercream in bright, jewel colours.

1 Sift the icing sugar into a big bowl. Add the butter. Beat until you have a smooth mixture.

Only remove the yellow layer – the white layer underneath tastes bitter.

2 Grate the zest from the outside of half the lemon, on the small holes of a grater. Cut the lemon in half and squeeze out the juice.

3 Add the lemon zest to the mixture. Sift over the flour. Stir it in. Add 1½ teaspoons of the lemon juice and mix. Squeeze the mixture into a ball.

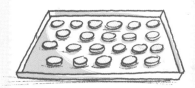

4 Put the ball on a lightly floured surface. Roll it with your hands to make a log around 2½cm (1in) across. Wrap it in plastic food wrap and put it in the fridge for 30 minutes.

5 Heat the oven to 180°C, 350°F or gas mark 4. Grease the baking tray (see page 36). Unwrap the log. Use a sharp knife to cut it into ½cm (¼in) slices.

6 Arrange the slices on the baking tray. Bake for 8-10 minutes, until they are turning golden. Leave the biscuits on the tray to cool completely.

7 To make the lemon buttercream, follow the instructions for citrus buttercream on page 15. Divide the buttercream into 3 equal parts. Spoon 2 parts into separate bowls.

8 Put a few drops of red and blue food dye in two of the bowls. Mix it in. Follow the instructions on page 49 to pipe small swirls of buttercream onto the biscuits.

9 Each time you change to a new shade of buttercream, wash the piping bag or gun (or use a fresh one) to keep the colours separate.

To make white buttercream like this, use the palest butter you can find.

You can make edible star and ball decorations like these using ready-to-roll icing – find out how on page 26.

Bright flower biscuits

Ingredients:

50g (2oz) softened butter, margarine or dairy-free spread

50g (2oz) caster sugar

1 medium egg

2 teaspoons milk or water

125g (4½oz) plain flour

15g (½oz) cornflour

around 12 see-through boiled sweets

You will also need a rolling pin, a baking tray, a clean tea towel and some medium-sized flower-shaped cookie cutters and small round or flower-shaped cookie cutters. If you're planning to hang up your biscuits, you will also need a wide drinking straw and some ribbon.

Makes around 12

These flower-shaped biscuits have see-through middles made from bright boiled sweets. You can hang them up for special occasions or parties.

1 Heat the oven to 180°C, 350°F or gas mark 4. Line the baking tray (see page 36). Put the butter and sugar in a big bowl. Beat until they're smooth.

Use the egg white in the macaroons on page 52.

2 Separate the egg, following the instructions on page 36. Mix the yolk into the butter and sugar mixture.

3 Add the milk or water, then sift on the flour and cornflour. Mix them in, then use your hands to squeeze the mixture into a ball.

4 Dust a clean work surface and rolling pin with a little flour. Roll out the dough until it's as thick as your little finger.

5 Use the medium-sized cutters to cut out lots of shapes. Use a spatula to lift the shapes onto the tray.

6 If you want to hang up your biscuits, make a hole near the edge of each shape by pressing the straw through it, like this.

7 Use the small cutters to cut a hole in the middle of each shape. Squeeze the scraps together, roll them out again and make more biscuits.

You could pipe icing onto your biscuits – see page 49.

If you hang up your biscuits, don't eat them afterwards, as they might be dirty.

8 Take a sweet. Leave it in its wrapper. Put it on a board. Cover it with the tea towel. Hit it with the rolling pin, to crush it into pieces. Take off the tea towel. Remove the wrapper.

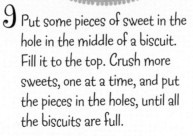

9 Put some pieces of sweet in the hole in the middle of a biscuit. Fill it to the top. Crush more sweets, one at a time, and put the pieces in the holes, until all the biscuits are full.

10 Bake for 12 minutes. Leave on the tray until completely cold. To hang them up, push a loop of ribbon through a hole. Push the ends of the ribbon through the loop and pull.

Yoyo biscuits

These round chocolate and vanilla sandwich biscuits look like little yoyos. They are rolled in sugar sprinkles, but you can leave them plain, if you like.

Ingredients:

175g (6oz) softened butter

40g (1½oz) icing sugar

1 teaspoon vanilla essence

175g (6oz) plain flour

40g (1½oz) cornflour

1 tablespoon cocoa powder

For the chocolate frosting:

40g (1½oz) butter

75g (3oz) plain or milk chocolate

You will also need 2 baking trays and some sugar sprinkles.

Makes around 12 pairs

These biscuits were all filled with chocolate frosting, but you could use buttercream (page 14) or butterscotch filling (page 55) instead.

1 Heat the oven to 190°C, 375°F or gas mark 5. Grease or line the baking trays (see page 36).

2 Put the butter in a big bowl. Sift on the icing sugar. Beat until it's smooth. Stir in the vanilla. Sift on the flour and cornflour. Mix well.

3 Put half the mixture in another bowl, sift on the cocoa and mix it in.

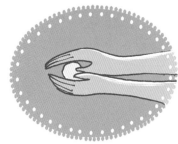

4 Take a teaspoon of one mixture. Use your hands to roll it into a ball. Put it on a baking tray. Make more balls. Space them well apart.

5 Use the back of a fork to flatten each of the balls, like this. Bake for 12-14 minutes.

6 Meanwhile, make the chocolate frosting (see page 15).

7 Leave the biscuits on the trays for a few minutes, then move them to a wire rack to cool completely.

8 When the biscuits are cool and the frosting is spreadable, spread frosting on half the biscuits. Press on the rest of the biscuits.

9 Spread some sugar sprinkles on a plate. Roll each biscuit sandwich in the sprinkles.

Piping and icing tips

Here are some tips on how to decorate cakes and cookies by spreading or piping on icing. You can make your own icing and then pipe it using an icing gun or piping bag, or you can buy writing icing in tubes ready for piping.

Flat icing

You can do this with buttercream or glacé icing (pages 14 and 15).

1 Use a blunt knife or the back of a spoon to spread a fairly thin layer of icing all over a cake or biscuit.

2 Fill a cup with warm water. Dip in the blade of a blunt knife. Wipe the knife on the edge of the cup to get rid of excess water.

3 Run the knife carefully over the surface of the icing, to make it smooth. Leave the icing to dry, unless you're going to use it for feather icing (see opposite page).

Rough icing

You can do this with buttercream or cream cheese frosting.

1 Use a blunt knife to spread a generous layer of icing all over a cake.

2 Drag and swirl the knife over the surface of the icing, making rough peaks.

A high, swirly topping

Ordinary liquid food dye is fine for tinting icing or buttercream in pale shades, but too much can make the icing or buttercream runny. For strong shades, use gel food dye instead.

Piping swirls

You will need a tube, gun or bag fitted with a star- or flower-shaped nozzle and filled with buttercream.

1 Hold the tube, gun or bag over a cake or biscuit. Squeeze until some icing comes out.

A small swirl

This biscuit was feather iced.

You can also use writing icing to pipe lines for feather icing.

2 To pipe a small swirl, squeeze until a swirl forms. Stop squeezing and lift the nozzle away quickly.

3 For a high, swirly topping, pipe a small swirl (see left). Then, pipe a spiral starting at the edge of the cake. Keep squeezing as you move the nozzle inwards and upwards, over the small swirl. Stop squeezing and lift the nozzle away quickly.

Piping lines or dots

You will need some writing icing, or a tube, gun or bag fitted with a small round nozzle and filled with glacé icing or buttercream.

1 Hold the tube, gun or bag over a cake or biscuit. Squeeze until a dot of icing comes out.

2 To pipe a dot, stop squeezing and lift the nozzle away quickly.

3 To pipe a line, follow step 1 above. Then, keep squeezing as you move the nozzle across the cake or biscuit, leaving a trail of icing in whatever shape you like. At the end, stop squeezing and lift the nozzle away quickly.

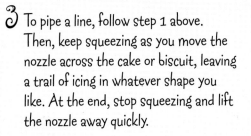

Feather icing

You will need glacé icing (page 15), a gun or bag fitted with a small round nozzle and filled with glacé icing in a contrasting shade, and a cocktail stick.

1 Flat ice a cake or biscuit (opposite). While the icing is still wet, pipe on some lines.

2 Drag the point of the cocktail stick across the lines, to make points. Move the stick along, then drag it across again, to make more points.

Lollipop cookies

Ingredients:

1 orange

50g (2oz) caster sugar

50g (2oz) softened butter, margarine or dairy-free spread

1 medium egg

125g (4½oz) plain flour

15g (½oz) cornflour

For the icing:

100g (4oz) icing sugar

different shades of food dye

You will also need a rolling pin, a round cookie cutter around 4cm (1½in) across, 2 baking trays, a pastry brush and around 12-15 wooden skewers.

Makes around 12-15

These chunky orange cookies are baked on sticks, then decorated with bright shades of icing, to look like old-fashioned lollipops.

1 Heat the oven to 180°C, 350°F or gas mark 4. Line the baking trays with parchment (see page 36).

Only remove the orange layer – the white layer underneath tastes bitter.

2 Grate the zest from the outside of the orange using the small holes of a grater. Squeeze the juice from half the orange and save it for later.

3 Put the zest in a big bowl. Add the sugar and butter. Beat until they're pale and fluffy.

4 Break the egg into a cup. Beat it with a fork (see page 9). Pour half of it into the big bowl and mix it in. Save the rest for later.

5 Sift on the flour and cornflour and mix them in. Then, use your hands to squeeze the mixture into a ball.

6 Dust a clean work surface and a rolling pin with flour. Roll out the dough (see page 37) until it is half as thick as your little finger.

7 Use the round cutter to cut out lots of circles. Squeeze the scraps together, roll them out again and cut more circles, until the dough is used up.

This cookie was flat iced, then decorated with a piped spiral.

This one was feather iced in yellow and pink.

These spots were piped with writing icing.

You could pipe decorations onto a cookie without flat icing it first.

Lollipop cookies

These cookies were made using 2 sizes of cutter.

8 Use a spatula to move half the circles onto the trays. Space them well apart, to leave room for the skewers.

9 Brush egg all over the circles on the tray. Put a skewer on each one. Lay another dough circle over each of the circles on the tray. Press them on gently.

10 Bake the cookies for 12-15 minutes, until they are golden. Leave them for 10 minutes, then move them carefully to a wire rack to cool.

11 To make the icing, sift the icing sugar into a bowl. Mix in 1 tablespoon of the orange juice you set aside earlier. Divide the icing between 3 or more small bowls.

12 Mix a few drops of food dye into each bowl of icing. Then, ice the cookies, following the instructions on pages 48-49 for flat icing, piping lines and dots, or feather icing.

Butterscotch macaroons

Ingredients:

For the macaroon shells:

50g (2oz) icing sugar

1 medium egg

1 pinch cream of tartar

15g (½oz) soft dark brown sugar

50g (2oz) ground almonds

For the butterscotch filling:

15g (½oz) butter

40g (1½oz) soft dark brown sugar

100g (4oz) full-fat cream cheese

You will also need a baking tray.

Makes around 6 pairs

These little macaroons have shells made from egg whites and ground almonds, filled with a creamy butterscotch filling. You'll find other flavours on the opposite page.

1 Line the baking tray with baking parchment (see page 36). Sift the icing sugar into a bowl. Take the cream cheese out of the fridge.

You don't need the yolk. You could use it in the flower biscuits on page 44.

2 Separate the egg (see page 36). Put the white in a large, clean bowl.

3 Whisk the egg white (see page 36) until it stays in a floppy point when you lift up the whisk.

4 Whisk in the cream of tartar and 1 tablespoon of the icing sugar. Add the rest of the icing sugar a tablespoon at a time, whisking well each time.

5 Sift the soft dark brown sugar and ground almonds into the bowl. Squash any soft lumps through with a spoon. Throw away any hard bits left in the sieve.

Move the spoon in the...

...shape of a number 8.

6 Use a metal spoon to fold everything together very gently.

Use another spoon to push off each blob.

7 Put a teaspoonful of the mixture on the tray. Make more blobs, spacing them out well. Tap the tray sharply on the work surface, twice.

A butterscotch macaroon

A lime macaroon

A strawberry macaroon

8 Leave the shells for 30 minutes. Meanwhile, make the butterscotch filling, following the instructions on page 55. Put it in a bowl in the fridge to chill.

9 Heat the oven to 110°C, 225°F or gas mark ¼. Bake for 30 minutes. Turn off the oven. Leave them in for 15 minutes, then take them out. Leave on the tray to cool.

10 Spread some filling on the flat side of a macaroon shell. Press on the flat side of another shell. Fill the rest in the same way.

Lime macaroons

To make the shells, replace the soft dark brown sugar with 15g (½oz) caster sugar and add a few drops of green food dye at the same time.

To make the filling, you will need 1 lime, 3 tablespoons full-fat cream cheese and 4 teaspoons icing sugar. Grate the zest from the lime. Squeeze the juice from the lime, too. Put the zest, 4 teaspoons of the juice and the cream cheese in a bowl. Sift on the icing sugar. Add a few drops of green food dye. Mix gently.

Strawberry macaroons

To make the shells, replace the soft dark brown sugar with 15g (½oz) caster sugar and add a few drops of pink or red food dye at the same time.

To make the filling, mix 1 tablespoon of smooth strawberry jam and 3 tablespoons of full-fat cream cheese in a bowl.

For a dairy-free filling, just use smooth strawberry jam on its own.

Toppings and fillings

Here you'll find instructions for making whipped cream and butterscotch filling, and decorating your little cakes and cookies with drizzled chocolate.

Whipped cream

1 Pour the double or whipping cream into a big bowl. Hold the bowl firmly with one hand. Use the other hand to beat the cream with a whisk as hard as you can.

Don't beat too much, or the cream will go hard.

2 Carry on beating until the cream becomes stiff. When you lift the whisk, the cream should stay in a floppy point.

Raspberry cream

You will need 150ml (¼ pint) double or whipping cream, 100g (4oz) fresh or defrosted frozen raspberries and 1 tablespoon of caster sugar.

1 Whip the cream following the instructions on the left, then put the raspberries and sugar in a bowl. Mash with a fork until the raspberries are squashed and juicy.

2 Tip the raspberries onto the whipped cream. Mix them in gently with a metal spoon, moving it in the shape of a number 8.

This little chocolate raspberry gateau (page 17) was filled with raspberry cream.

Raspberry cream

Butterscotch filling

You will need 15g (½oz) butter, 40g (1½oz) soft dark brown sugar and 100g (4oz) full-fat cream cheese.

1 Put the butter and sugar in a pan. Put it over a low heat. Keep stirring until the butter melts and the sugar dissolves.

2 Take the pan off the heat. Add the cream cheese. Beat with a wooden spoon to mix it in. Leave to cool for 5 minutes.

Melting chocolate

You will need a heatproof bowl that fits snugly in a saucepan. The bottom of the bowl shouldn't touch the bottom of the pan.

1 Fill the pan with water to a depth of around 4cm (1½in). Put it over a medium heat. When the water bubbles, take it off the heat.

2 Break your chocolate into chunks. Put it in the bowl. Wearing oven gloves, lower the bowl into the pan. Leave for 5 minutes. Stir until the chocolate melts.

Drizzling chocolate

1 First, melt some chocolate following the instructions above. Then, scoop up some chocolate on a spoon.

2 Hold the spoon over your cake or cookie. Tip the spoon, then move it over the cake or cookie in a zigzag shape, leaving a trail of chocolate.

Butterscotch macaroons
— see page 52

Soft dark brown sugar

Butterscotch filling

Contains peanuts

Chocolate peanut bites

Ingredients:

50g (2oz) salted, roasted peanuts

100g (4oz) butter, softened

100g (4oz) caster sugar

50g (2oz) soft light brown sugar

100g (4oz) smooth peanut butter

½ teaspoon vanilla essence

1 medium egg

150g (5oz) plain flour

50g (2oz) plain, milk or white chocolate

You will also need 2 baking trays and some kitchen foil.

Makes around 35

These little biscuits are made with peanut butter. Each one has a dimple filled with chocolate and topped with a peanut – or you could use other nuts.

1 Heat the oven to 180°C, 350°F or gas mark 4. Line the baking trays (see page 36). Put the peanuts in a sieve. Rinse under a cold tap to remove the salt. Pat dry with a clean tea towel. Set aside.

2 Put the butter, caster sugar and soft light brown sugar in a bowl. Beat until you have a pale and fluffy mixture.

3 Stir in the peanut butter and vanilla. Then, break the egg into a cup, beat it with a fork and stir it into the mixture, too.

A blanched almond

White chocolate

4 Sift the flour onto the mixture in the bowl. Stir it in well, then use your hands to pat and squeeze the mixture into a ball.

5 Take a teaspoonful of the mixture. Use your hands to roll it into a ball. Put it on a tray. Make more balls, until the mixture is used up. Bake for 10-12 minutes, until golden.

6 While the biscuits are baking, take a small square of kitchen foil. Scrunch it into a ball around 2cm (1in) wide. Pinch one end to make a handle.

7 Take the biscuits out of the oven. Hold the foil ball by its handle. Push it gently into the middle of each biscuit, to make a shallow dimple. The biscuits will crack a little as you do this.

8 Leave the biscuits to cool. Then, melt the chocolate (page 55). Spoon a little into the dimple in each biscuit. Top with the peanuts you set aside earlier.

Other flavours

Instead of peanuts, you could top your bites with shelled pistachios, macadamia nuts, or blanched almonds or hazelnuts. If the nuts are unsalted, you don't need to rinse them in step 1.

Instead of chocolate, you could fill the dimples in your biscuits with the butterscotch filling from page 55. Or, for really nutty bites, fill them with chocolate hazelnut spread.

The dimple on this biscuit was filled with butterscotch filling – see page 55.

Stripy biscuits

Ingredients:

For the vanilla dough:

25g (1oz) icing sugar

50g (2oz) butter, softened

3 rounded tablespoons plain flour

1 teaspoon milk

1 teaspoon vanilla essence

For the chocolate dough:

25g (1oz) icing sugar

1 tablespoon cocoa powder

50g (2oz) butter, softened

3 rounded tablespoons plain flour

2 teaspoons milk

For the mint dough:

25g (1oz) icing sugar

50g (2oz) butter, softened

1 teaspoon peppermint essence

¼ teaspoon green food dye

3 rounded tablespoons plain flour

½ teaspoon milk

You will also need a rolling pin, a pastry brush and 2 baking trays.

Makes around 25

These little square biscuits have stripes made from vanilla, chocolate and mint dough. You roll out the dough and then stack and slice it to make the stripes.

1 For the vanilla dough, sift the icing sugar into a bowl. Add the butter. Beat until smooth. Sift on the flour and add the milk and vanilla. Mix.

2 For the chocolate dough, sift the icing sugar and cocoa into a bowl. Add the butter. Beat until smooth. Sift on the flour, add the milk and mix.

3 For the mint dough, sift the icing sugar into a bowl. Add the butter, peppermint essence and food dye. Beat until smooth. Sift on the flour and add the milk. Mix.

4 Use your hands to pat, squeeze and roll each of the mixtures into a log shape around 8cm (3in) long. Wrap them in plastic food wrap. Put them in the fridge for 30 minutes.

5 Sprinkle flour on a clean work surface and a rolling pin. Roll the rolling pin over one of the logs, to make a rectangle around 8cm (3in) wide and 15cm (6in) long.

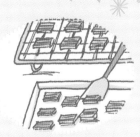

6 Roll out the other two lugs in the same way. Brush a little water over one strip of dough. Lift another strip on top. Brush it with water, then lift on the third strip.

7 Cut off any wavy edges. Cut the stack in half lengthways, like this. Brush the top of one stack with water. Lift the other stack on top and pat it gently so it sticks on.

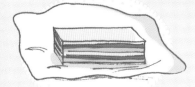

8 Very gently, wrap the dough in plastic food wrap and put it on a tray. Put it in the fridge to chill for 30 minutes.

9 Heat the oven to 180°C, 350°F or gas mark 4. Grease the baking trays (see page 36).

10 Unwrap the dough. Using a sharp knife, cut it into ½cm (¼in) slices. Put the slices on the baking trays.

11 Bake for 12-15 minutes. Leave the biscuits for 2 minutes to cool a little, then use a spatula to move them to a wire rack, to cool completely.

Mini chocolate chip cookies

Ingredients:

1 large lemon

75g (3oz) softened butter,
  margarine or dairy-free spread

75g (3oz) caster sugar

75g (3oz) soft light brown sugar

1 medium egg

175g (6oz) plain flour

½ teaspoon baking powder

150g (5oz) white chocolate chips

For decorating:

100g (4oz) white chocolate

Makes around 40

These little, soft cookies have lemon dough and white chocolate chips, but you can make classic chocolate chip and other flavours – see the opposite page.

Only remove the yellow layer – the white layer underneath tastes bitter.

1 Heat the oven to 180°C, 350°F or gas mark 4. Grease two baking trays (see page 36). Grate the zest from the outside of the lemon, using the small holes of a grater. Then, squeeze the juice from half the lemon.

3 Break the egg into a small bowl. Beat with a fork. Add it to the big bowl a little at a time, beating well each time. Add 1 teaspoon of lemon juice and mix that in, too.

2 Put the lemon zest, butter, margarine or spread, caster sugar and soft light brown sugar in a big bowl. Beat them until the mixture is smooth.

4 Sift the flour and baking powder into the bowl. Stir the mixture until it is smooth. Add the white chocolate chips and stir them in.

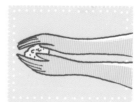

5 Take a half teaspoon of the mixture and use your hands to roll it into a ball. Put the ball of dough on a tray and flatten it slightly.

6 Make more cookies in the same way with the rest of the mixture. Bake for 10 minutes, until golden. Leave the cookies on the trays for a few minutes.

7 Use a spatula to lift the cookies onto a wire rack to cool. When they have cooled, melt the white chocolate and drizzle it over them (see page 55).

Other flavours

For classic chocolate chip cookies, leave out the lemon and use plain or milk chocolate chips. At step 3, add 1 teaspoon vanilla essence instead of the lemon juice.

Instead of the lemon, you could use 1 orange or 2 limes.

For chocolate dough, use just 150g (5oz) flour. Sift in 4 tablespoons cocoa powder with the flour in step 4.

Index

Allergy advice

Many of the recipes in this book already have suggestions in the ingredients lists for allergy-free ingredients you can substitute, for example using dairy-free spread instead of butter. The list below tells you about any ingredients that can't be substituted, but might be a problem for those who can't eat wheat, gluten, dairy, egg or nuts.

If you're cooking for someone with food allergies, you should use allergy-free chocolate, which is free from wheat, gluten, egg, nuts and, sometimes, dairy. You should also check any packaged ingredients, such as vanilla essence, cocoa powder or sugar sprinkles, to make sure they don't contain anything unsuitable.

Tiny cupcakes
Contain wheat, gluten and egg.

Small strawberry sponge cakes
Contain wheat, gluten and egg.

Little chocolate cherry gateaux
Contain wheat, gluten, dairy and egg. The raspberry and hazelnut versions can be made dairy-free. The hazelnut version contains nuts.

Mini éclairs
Contain wheat, gluten, dairy and egg.

Tiny citrus cakes
Contain wheat, gluten and egg.

Little red velvet cakes
Contain wheat, gluten and dairy.

Chocolate orange cakepops
Contain wheat, gluten, dairy and egg. For a dairy-free version, use dairy-free chocolate for the frosting and coating.

Iced fancies
Contain wheat, gluten, dairy and egg.

Little coconut cakes
Contain coconut, wheat, gluten, dairy and egg. Coconut may not be suitable for nut allergy sufferers.

Upside-down berry cakes
Contain egg.

Ginger biscuits
Contain wheat, gluten and dairy.

Shortbread fingers
Contain wheat, gluten and dairy. A gluten-free version is included.

Little gem biscuits
Contain wheat, gluten and dairy.

Bright flower biscuits
Contain wheat, gluten and egg.

Yoyo biscuits
Contain wheat, gluten and dairy.

Lollipop cookies
Contain wheat, gluten and egg.

Butterscotch macaroons
Contain dairy, egg and nuts. The strawberry version can be made dairy-free.

Chocolate peanut bites
Contain wheat, gluten, dairy, egg and peanuts.

Stripy biscuits
Contain wheat, gluten and dairy.

Mini chocolate chip cookies
Contain wheat, gluten, dairy and egg. For a dairy-free version, use dairy-free white chocolate.

Art Director: Mary Cartwright   Senior Designer: Helen Lee
Digital imaging by Nick Wakeford
With thanks to Fiona Patchett